RETAIL
Rules!

RETAIL Rules!

52 ways to achieve retail success

by **KEVIN COUPE**
illustrated by **STEVE HICKNER**

BRIGANTINE MEDIA

Illustrations by Steve Hickner

Brigantine Media
211 North Avenue, St. Johnsbury, Vermont 05819
Phone: 802-751-8802 | Fax: 802-751-8804
Email: neil@brigantinemedia.com
Website: www.brigantinemedia.com

ISBN 978-1-9384064-1-6

Printed in Canada

Dedication

For Laura, who knows one of the first rules of true love—when to give me a hug and when to give me a kick in the rear end.

And for David, Brian, and Ali, who I hope can look past my shortcomings as a father to see the love and admiration I feel for them.

The Rules

The Rules

I'VE NEVER BEEN a big rules guy. Just ask the nuns at Saints John and Paul Elementary School, for whom breaking my spirit, making me obedient, and turning me into a rule-follower seemed less like a job and more like a divine calling.

I've been writing about retailing for thirty years—for the last thirteen years on my blog, *MorningNewsBeat.com*. I worked my way through high school and college, and to supplement a meager reporter's income afterwards, in several retail stores. And I've had the great opportunity to meet some wonderful retailers—and by this, I mean wonderful people who happen to be retailers—over the years.

Retailing is a tough journey, and they keep changing the road map. It's difficult, if not impossible, to know what the next right move is (though some folks would settle simply for not making a next *disastrous* move). This book provides a little bit of guidance for getting through the terrain—common sense, easily applied rules, rooted in real-world business.

The rules are short. The sentiments, simple. The examples, I hope, are evocative. The illustrations, by the estimable Steve Hickner, make the whole experience a lot more fun.

I've tried to spread the examples around, using lots of different retailers as models for what—and sometimes what *not*—to do. But I'll concede right now that names like Amazon, Apple, Starbucks, and Netflix pop up a lot. They should. They're game-changers. They raise the level of competition in their categories, and they provide lots of ideas for big and small retailers alike.

One thing. While I've learned many of these rules from people I admire, and crafted others from what I've seen and heard over the years, let's be clear. These rules reflect my biases, priorities, and experience.

You may have 52 different ones.

If so, that's okay. This is a rule book even for people who don't like rules.

Besides, I've never been a big rules guy anyway.

KC

PART ONE

Management

Have a vision.

LEADERSHIP SHOULD BE able to sum up its goals for a retail entity in one sentence. Or a couple of short sentences. Really short sentences.

That's vision.

As in ...

"To be the world's most respected and successful designer, manufacturer and retailer of the finest jewelry."
—Tiffany & Co.

"To be the premier quality food retailer in the world."
—Publix Super Markets

"Our vision is to be earth's most customer centric company; to build a place where people can come to

find and discover anything they might want to buy online."
—Amazon

"Our goal is to provide outstanding service every day, one customer at a time."
—Nordstrom

"We treat strangers like friends and friends like family."
—Bob Evans

A strong vision sums up priorities in just a few words. The vision may have to do with products, or employees, or customer service. But this simple statement is like the North Star—a fixed point that allows you to navigate successfully through almost any situation.

Manage for Main Street, not Wall Street.

I'M NOT HERE to suggest that the investor class should be ignored. Far from it.

I'd argue, however, that in these times of intense and increased competition, investors and analysts, as well as boards of directors, need to adjust their expectations about CEO priorities when creating a successful and sustainable business model.

Jim Sinegal, the former chairman/CEO of Costco, always said that he was not going to pay attention when analysts suggested that if he would just raise prices a bit, increase margins a smidge, and pay his people a little bit less, he could boost profits, which would result in a higher per-share price.

No, Sinegal said. His job was to make sure

shoppers would continue to buy from Costco, which meant keeping prices as sharp as possible, and to make sure that employees were buying into the Costco vision, which meant paying them a living wage and providing generous benefits.

Take care of Main Street, Sinegal said, and Wall Street will take care of itself. (He was right.)

Tactics are different from strategy.

I ONCE SAT through a regional retailer's meeting about strategy and tactics. As an outsider, I was hired to serve as a "B. S." detector (their phrase), keeping them honest and focused about what needed to be done.

The company's CEO stood up and said, "Today, we're going to lay out 137 strategies for how we are going succeed in the coming year."

I raised my hand.

He looked at me, surprised. "Already?"

"Yup," I said. "You can't have 137 strategies. And even if you did, there is no way you can act on them all in one year. Most great companies have a few strategic imperatives, and then create tactics through which those strategies are implemented."

The vast majority of the company's "strategies"

were, in fact, tactics (134 of them, if I recall correctly).

Do you know the difference between strategies and tactics?

"Improve customer service" is a strategic goal. "Have checkout personnel greet customers by name whenever possible" is a tactic you employ to reach that goal.

"Get customers to come into the store more often" is a strategic goal. "Create a loyalty program" is a tactic.

"Encourage customers to purchase more each visit" is a strategic goal. "Cross merchandise" is a tactic.

Get the difference?

The fish stinks from the head(quarters).

THIS ONE IS inspired by one of the world's iconic retailers, Feargal Quinn, founder of the Superquinn chain of supermarkets in Ireland.

From the beginning, Feargal established that Superquinn's main office would not be known as "headquarters."

Nope. In fact, if anyone on the executive team referred to that office as "headquarters," they had to pay a small fine.

Rather, that building—where all the top executives had desks and chairs and conference rooms—was officially known as the "Superquinn Support Office."

Because that's what they did: *Support* the stores.

Feargal understood that a headquarters-centric retail business was one that by its very nature

would have inappropriate priorities. By formalizing the company's priorities in two words—"Support Office"—he made sure that everybody's eyes were on the right ball.

Timing is everything.

RETAILING IS KIND of like surfing. You have to catch the wave in just the right way, or you fail.

Consider the case of Borders in 2001, which didn't understand the then-nascent appeal of e-commerce. Rather than investing in it, Borders decided to outsource its online business to a little Seattle company called Amazon.

Or the case of Circuit City, which totally misread the marketplace—it opened too many stores throughout the 2000s; it stopped paying commissions to salespeople in 2003, who then stopped being as productive; and it became reactive to the marketplace

with little evidence of innovation. It missed the tsunami created by the Apple Store.

Or the case of Blockbuster, which was so consumed with building its video rental business with stores around the country that it missed the competitive threats from new companies like Netflix in 1997 and Redbox in 2002.

Compare this to Staples, which is trying to remain relevant today by upgrading its online business, closing unproductive stores, offering in-store pickup the same day as products are ordered online, and rolling out touch-screen kiosks in stores to offer a broader array of products.

It is too early to know whether Staples will succeed, or if it is too late. But unlike Borders, Circuit City, and Blockbuster, it is still out there, paddling away, trying to catch the wave.

Make sure you have a big enough boat.

I CO-WROTE A book in 2010 about using movie metaphors in business. (*The Big Picture: Essential Business Lessons from the Movies.*)

I think this is one of the best lessons from that book, and one that every retailer should keep in mind.

The movie is *Jaws*, which is a great business movie because it is all about denial.

The mayor is in denial: despite the shark, he wants to keep the beaches open because it is the tourist season. (The shark thinks "tourist season" is the same as "lunch.") Quint, the shark hunter, played by Robert Shaw, is in denial: he wants to hunt the shark by himself. Hooper, the young marine biologist played by Richard Dreyfuss, keeps getting into the water with the shark, and police chief Brody, played by Roy Scheider, doesn't swim, hates the water, but lives on an island.

Everybody is in denial until that moment in the movie when, while tossing chum into the water, Brody sees the shark for the first time and says, "We're going to need a bigger boat."

In every retail situation, you have to have the right strategy, right tactics, right vision, right people, and right technology if you are going to succeed. In other words, you have to have a big enough boat.

If your store has a great selection and lousy employees, you can be eaten by better competition. Or, if you have great people but mediocre merchandise, same thing. Or, if you have great products and great people, but you are doing nothing to understand your customers better, the competition can take you.

Make sure you have a big enough boat.

Read more than just trade journals.

IN THE LATE 1980s and early '90s, I worked as a writer for a trade magazine, running its small video division. I was the only person at the time who had a computer hooked up to the Internet. I used AOL to access information, and even started placing orders on Amazon. (I was so early to the Amazon party that one Christmas they sent me a coffee mug, just to say thank you for being a customer. Yikes!)

I suggested to my boss that we had a unique opportunity to corner the market as an information source for our industry by making all of our stuff available online.

That idea went nowhere. They decided to double down on print magazines. Within months the video division was shut down and I was laid off.

They missed the Internet boat. It isn't that I'm that smart, but I was reading new magazines like *Wired*, *Red Herring*, and *Fast Company*, while my bosses were reading trade journals. They couldn't see what I saw, because they were looking in the wrong place.

Whatever industry you work in, don't just read the trade journals. They are in business to tell you what you probably already know about your industry.

It's like only eating vanilla ice cream, or spaghetti with butter. You may get full, but you aren't expanding your palate.

Travel.

YOU HAVE TO get out and see stuff. It doesn't matter how big or small your retail business is. The best way to learn is to get in a car or on a plane and go see what other people are doing. Not just in your town, but throughout the United States and abroad.

If you are in the clothing business, don't just look at clothing stores. If you are in the food business, don't just look at food stores. Look at everything. Educate yourself.

There are food retailers who make a habit of sending their people to travel to Italy and France to learn how people make cheese and wine, because it allows them to educate their shoppers better back home. At Metropolitan Markets in Seattle, and Zupan's in Portland, Oregon, they make an effort to look at stores all over the country and the world, and constantly bring back ideas that make them more differentiated and competitive.

Build these kinds of trips into your budget, and make it one of the things that you evaluate people on: what stores they saw and what ideas they got from looking at them, with bonus points for "out of the box" thinking.

Visit the competition.

ONE OF THE best ideas that I've run into in the retail business is the creation of "share groups," which allow non-competing retailers in the same retail segment from different parts of the country to get together a couple of times a year to share ideas, programs, successes, and, yes, failures. When they get together, often in the home market of one of the members, they usually spend at least one day touring all the interesting retailers in that market.

Without fail, this trip turns into a highlight of the meeting, because people are actually seeing what the competition is doing. What merchandise they are carrying. How they display it. How they price it. How they cross-merchandise it with other products. What kind of lighting they use. What kind of check-out systems they use. How their employees interact with customers. And more. It's the kind of information that can only be gleaned by actually going into other retailers' stores.

Visit your direct competition in your marketplace. You need to know exactly what they are doing that's better, worse, and the same as you. It needn't be antagonistic—don't bring a camera crew and a large group of employees. But keep tabs on what your direct competitors are up to, and do it regularly, so you aren't blind-sided by something new.

Worried that your customers might see you there? Don't be. You might learn something from them, too . . .

Years ago I was doing a magazine piece about a Missouri retailer named Dave Trottier, and after we looked at his stores, he took me to see the competition. He wanted me to see what he thought he was doing better, and the stuff that he thought he could learn from.

While we were there, we bumped into one of his regular customers, who was a little nonplussed to see Trottier there. "What are you doing here?" she said. "Never mind that," he replied. "What are *you* doing here?" And then they had a long conversation, Trottier took copious notes, and he walked away with an understanding of what had lured away someone he thought was one of his most loyal shoppers and what he needed to do to bring her back.

She may have started off the conversation embarrassed, but I'm sure she ended it feeling valued. And valuable.

Kill the sacred cows.

SOME PEOPLE EQUATE sacred cows with core business values. Often, however, they are just business practices with lots of dust on them.

Beau Fraser, managing director at The Gate Worldwide, a global advertising agency, is co-author of one of my favorite business books: *Death to All Sacred Cows: How Successful Business People Put the Old Rules Out to Pasture.* (It is a book I wish I'd written, if only for the title.)

Beau defines sacred cows this way: "The rules, approaches, formulas, standards, and cues businesses follow for no better reason than that's the way things have always been done. Businesses that only look to the past to guide their futures are doomed to failure."

Consider RadioShack, which is a poster child for hanging on to outmoded sacred cows. This company could have been at the epicenter of the technology revolution, having been a purveyor of radio parts, CB radios, and computer components. But its stores have not changed fundamentally in years, despite how much the world of technology has changed.

When it tried to adjust, its efforts usually were too little, too late, or too poorly conceived. It was attempting to survive in an innovation-driven world without being innovative itself. RadioShack's sacred cows had no value in the modern world.

Mark Twain put it this way: "Sacred cows make the best hamburger."

I couldn't have said it any better.

Disrupt from within.

NETFLIX KEEPS CHALLENGING its own business model from within. When it was just getting started, Netflix CEO Reed Hastings said that his company was not in the DVD rental business, but rather, in the entertainment delivery business . . . and that it would embrace and adapt whatever technologies and processes that would keep it relevant to the consumer.

Netflix is shifting from physical DVDs to a streaming model to keep its entertainment delivery in step with current technology. But now it is also in the entertainment *creation* business. Netflix has

developed its own programming—like "House of Cards"—that serves as a private label line of differentiated content. You can't get it anywhere else, so if you like "House of Cards" or other Netflix series, you're going to stay hooked into the Netflix system.

Amazon is developing its own differentiated programming; it has a new series in 2014, "Transparent," that is so good that some critics are saying Amazon will have trouble living up to the standard it has set. And Google has plans to do much the same thing.

You have to keep disrupting from within. Otherwise, it'll be the competition that disrupts your business.

All in.

RETAILING IS A tough game, requiring enormous commitment. There's no room for people who are not totally committed to what needs to be done.

In my early twenties, I worked for a retailer that, after a couple of years of success, began to struggle. He taught me a lot, but when times got tough, he lost focus. He'd be absent for hours at a time, leaving me to run the place all by myself. Eventually, the business folded.

Compare that to the story of Lisa Sedlar, a former executive at Whole Foods, former CEO of New Seasons Markets, and currently the founder/CEO of Green Zebra, which might best be defined as a health-oriented convenience store. Think of it as a 7-Eleven built by Whole Foods, a potentially great idea. But she's in a tough, competitive marketplace and is working hard to get more people in the front door. Lisa spends virtually all her time in the store, and when she's not in the store, she's talking to potential backers. She's exhausted. All the time. She's even developed an eye twitch. (I'm not telling tales out of school here. She did a TED talk about this.)

But you know something? Lisa is all in. Totally focused. Completely passionate. And willing to put everything on the line to make her retail business a success.

Retailing requires nothing less.

PART TWO

Marketing

"Compete" is a verb.

THERE'S A SMALL liquor store that specializes in unique and fine wines. The folks who work there are knowledgeable, and its customers tend to be satisfied and reasonably loyal.

A customer went into this store the day before Mother's Day and found the shelves only two-thirds full. When he chose a bottle to give as a present, the customer was told that the store did not have any wrapping paper.

Apparently, the owners and staff were too busy focusing on a charity event to remember it was Mother's Day weekend. On Mother's Day itself, the store was closed. Lots of other stores in town were open, and everybody else seemed to be doing plenty of business selling wine, flowers, and whatnot.

This wine shop forgot how to compete.

"Compete" is a verb. It requires action, not passivity. You have to be vigilant, aggressive, and alert.

Here's how the wine shop could have actively competed for business:

- Start by being open on Mother's Day.
- For a month in advance, publicize Mother's Day hours with cards placed in every bag.
- Reiterate the Mother's Day hours via e-mail that weekend.
- Partner with a local candy or flower retailer to create Mother's Day gift baskets only available at the wine shop.
- Champagne tasting that weekend to get people in the mood.
- Maybe a contest, with some lucky customer's mom chosen to get a case of wine as a prize.
- And certainly, appropriate wrapping paper.

In other words, work overtime to be competitive. You can't cede business to other retailers, because those retailers will find ways to keep customers coming back for more.

You don't have a right to be in business. You have to earn it.

Narratives sell.

PEOPLE ARE WIRED to communicate with stories. Plenty of researchers have established the connection between storytelling and brain activity. Some of the best retailers have learned how to take advantage of our love of narratives.

That's what the Disney Store did in its heyday. Or what the Apple Store continues to do. Or what REI does. Or Vineyard Vines. Or Costco.

These stores have a tale to tell, and the minute you walk in, you understand what they are all about.

At Vineyard Vines, it is about how two guys, fed up with the corporate world, decided to start selling ties . . . and expanded into a men's and women's clothing retailer/manufacturer with a specific world view. (It has a lot to do with boats.)

At REI, you see the climbing wall, and you know exactly what the story is. You're not just buying outdoors clothing and equipment . . . you're investing in a lifestyle.

At Costco, the message from the moment you step in the front door is that you're about to go on a treasure hunt . . . so be prepared to spend more money that you planned. (Somehow, this ends up being okay, because you're finding new treats.)

Compare this to stores like Sears or Kmart, where there seems to be little thought given to the retail story, and the experience is haphazard.

"Tell me a story," is one of the first sentences children utter. As we get older, the desire for narratives doesn't flag.

Tell your customers a story.

Local sells.

I WAS VISITING friends, Robin Russell and Dave Grooters, owners of Carlton Cellars vineyard and tasting room in Carlton, Oregon. They gave me a tour of their facility and invited me up to the house for lunch. We sat on the deck, drinking wine from the vineyards that spread out below us, eating sandwiches that they'd picked up from a local deli. My sandwich was what I can only describe as the best BLT I'd ever tasted.

I told them so, suspicious that I was simply being seduced by the wine and the moment.

Dave laughed. "It should be good," he said. "The bacon came from the pigs on a farm just down the road."

In that instant, I became a "local" convert.

"Local" can mean a lot of things. It can mean the pig farm down the road, or the apple orchard ten miles away. It also can mean "made in the USA"—which is why New Balance tries to make as many running shoes in the United States as possible, why Apple is moving some of its manufacturing onto American soil, and why Walmart has pledged to spend billions on American-made items.

"Local" is an economic statement and a political statement. But it also is a feel-good statement. There is a growing interest on the part of many shoppers to know where things come from. When something is local, it allows both the merchant and the supplier to tell a story about the product. (See Rule 14: "Narratives sell.")

I refer you to the Saturday Farmers Market at Portland State University in Oregon, or any farmers market where local purveyors do exceptional business selling products and telling stories. There's a reason the farmers market industry is growing.

"Local" sells.

Sampling works.

THINK ABOUT THE last time you went to Costco. How much food did you eat as you were walking around the store?

I'll bet a lot. Because Costco always has known a basic food retailing rule:

> *If it smells good and tastes good, the odds are pretty good that the customer is going to buy it.*

Sampling is a great way to encourage customers to buy.

But what about retailers not in the food business?

There are ways to sample products or offer freebies, especially for your best customers who you want to

make sure don't wander off into the competition's stores.

Many tennis shops (online and bricks-and-mortar) allow people to test several racquets before buying them. For a minimal price at Home Depot, you can get an eight-ounce jar of paint to try on your wall before you commit to gallons.

New Balance has long had a program of "testers." They are frequent buyers of New Balance products who get sneakers sent to them from time to time. All that's asked is for them to wear the sneakers a lot, fill out a survey, and then send them back. What a great way to keep customers from trying Nike!

Take a tip from food stores and give your customers a sample.

Use theater.

THERE IS NOTHING like retail theater. It captures the imagination, brings people back time and again, and generates sales.

There are lots of examples, from the ridiculous to the sublime.

Stew Leonard's, a four-store supermarket chain in the New York metro area, has done it with everything from people in cow costumes who wander around giving people cookie samples, to installing a real beehive so customers can see how fresh honey is made.

At Jungle Jim's, an Ohio food retailer, owner Jim Bonaminio has installed enormous fish tanks where various breeds of fish swim around, to give his customers access to the freshest possible fish. It's like a trip to the aquarium!

Sometimes theater can be architectural—think of the flagship Apple Stores, where the combination of glass and marble and clean, modern design send a compelling message about what the store and company stand for.

Retail theater can go hand-in-hand with transparency (see Rule 23, "Be transparent."). Consider the open back rooms featured by some supermarkets and restaurants, which allow customers to watch the food prep. That's theater . . . and it can be bottom-line effective.

When the curtain rises, the idea is to engage the customer/audience. When the curtain comes down, the idea is to have made the sale.

Bravo!

Be a resource for information.

HERE'S A BASIC fact about retailing that most people in the business don't like to concede:

> *There's very little that a retailer sells*
> *that is absolutely unique to that retailer.*

In many cases, the competition sells identical brands for similar prices. Or, in the case of private label items, there are similar items on the shelves of competitors' stores. If these items are not available at the competitor's store down the street, they're almost certainly available online from someone.

So what do you do?

Be a resource for information in addition to being

a source of product. If customers know they can turn to you for that little bit of extra information, or some nugget of context or advice, it can be the differential advantage that keeps them returning to your store instead of going someplace else.

I liken it to the difference between using a GPS system and getting directions from someone who knows the area. The GPS will tell you how to get someplace using cold, analytical algorithms. But the person who knows the area . . . well, they can tell you about shortcuts, traffic problems, good and bad neighborhoods, where to stop for coffee. They can turn the act of getting from here to there into an experience.

That's why it makes sense for retailers like Sur la Table and Williams-Sonoma to offer cooking classes.

That's what a great retailer needs to do.

First   **Best**   **Different**

Be first, best, different.

IN DIRECT OPPOSITION to Rule 18, there are retailers who make it their business to find or create products that are "first, best, and different."

A great example is the father-and-daughter team of Rudy Dory and Lauren Johnson of Newport Avenue Market in Bend, Oregon. They seek out products that no one else carries and that people will know are carried only by Newport Avenue Market. (Check out their olive oil selection. Or their beer cooler. Or their specialty grocery aisles. I've been doing this a long time, and there are labels there I've never seen or heard of before.)

Their one-store operation is surrounded by

intimidating chain competition. Rudy and Lauren understand that finding unique products is an ongoing challenge; it's not like they ever can congratulate themselves on being done and take the rest of the week off.

Even their competition knows how good Rudy and Lauren are at this. Employees at some of the chain stores will, when they don't have an item that someone is looking for, refer them to Newport Avenue Market. (Grudgingly, I'm sure.)

First, best, different . . . three words that can translate to retail success.

Don't get boxed in.

WHEN IT COMES to retailing, one size definitely does not fit all.

Competitive retailers ought to figure out how to build different kinds of stores that will appeal to different kinds of customers . . . and then bring those stores, when appropriate, even to unorthodox locations *where the customers are.*

Starbucks is a great recent example of how to do this. In recent months, the company has announced that it is developing its own food truck program, sending them to select college campuses to satisfy caffeine-craving students who may not have a convenient coffee shop near campus. And it plans to test a small Express Starbucks in New York City.

Walmart has decided that being big isn't enough anymore, so it is testing a number of small store formats, and is even trying to run a convenience store concept on a number of college campuses.

Target is doing exactly the same thing. And the supermarket chain Hy-Vee has been very successful running convenience stores in addition to its main supermarket business.

Lunds/Byerly's, one of the best supermarket chains in the Midwest, has two different formats based on neighborhoods. Its Lunds stores tend to be a little smaller and a little more urban; its Byerly's stores bigger and more suburban in style. One of the company's most interesting units is its Lunds & Byerlys Kitchen, which is almost all fresh food—virtually no packaged grocery—and an eat-in restaurant, which is used to test concepts that can be exported to other, larger formats.

Most large hotel chains use different formats so that they can extend their footprints and grow their market shares. Marriott has sixteen different brands, and its CEO says their customers tell them they are tired of same-old, same-old beige rooms.

Sure, operating a different kind of store can be a marketing and merchandising challenge. But if you don't, you might miss out on opportunities.

Then, you'll find yourself boxed in. And that box will get smaller, and smaller, and smaller . . .

Good enough is never good enough.

I WAS LEADING a group of accomplished supermarket retailers on store tours of supermarkets in New England. One of our visits was to a retailer that is well known for its fresh foods and restaurant-quality meals, which in the supermarket industry is considered a real competitive advantage.

But very few of these retailers were impressed. We tasted lots of the food they were selling—sandwiches, pizza, Chinese food—and the general agreement was that it was "good enough."

That wasn't a compliment.

One of the retailers said the store seemed to be coasting on reputation, and that its expansion outside its home market might have caused it to lose a step or two. He noticed spotlights that weren't pointing at food, and a slight sense of ennui that seemed to pervade the premises. The customers didn't know it—yet—but the other retailers could feel it.

This happens to a lot of retailers. It isn't that they *intend* to mail it in, but at a certain point, routine takes over.

Good enough is *never* good enough, because it gives somebody else room to be better.

Nurture your brand equity.

WHEN IT COMES to retail brand equity, there are few cautionary tales as sobering as that of Krispy Kreme.

Little more than a decade ago, Krispy Kreme was one of the coolest retail brands out there. People would drive for miles and wait for the light to go on that signified hot doughnuts had just emerged from the oven, with almost the same level of expectation of the crowds that gather in the courtyard of the Vatican to wait for white smoke.

Management saw dollar signs in the popularity of the doughnuts. They started making Krispy Kreme doughnuts available everywhere. Supermarkets. Convenience stores. Gas stations. Office supply stores. The ubiquity of the product made it a little less special. Plus, the boxed doughnuts weren't warm, and as they cooled, they lost a little bit of their magic.

The folks at Krispy Kreme didn't understand

their brand equity—what made them special. So they undermined the whole value proposition.

Then, the low-carb fad hit.

Krispy Kreme no longer had the kind of brand equity that might have kept it growing even in adverse times, and the company was in disarray because of franchisee issues. The business fell faster than a doughnut without yeast.

Brand equity is something to be nurtured. Just because you *can* open stores doesn't necessarily mean you *should* open stores.

The folks at the Container Store have this right. There are some sixty stores in twenty states, but I suspect the company has been wooed by lots of real estate developers who would love to have a Container Store as an anchor tenant. At least some of the cachet of the Container Store comes from the fact that it's not everywhere, and that you have to make an effort to go to one of the stores.

The company is nurturing the brand, and from all appearances, doing so successfully.

Brand equity is not dependent on the number of store locations. It is about understanding the business's core values and value proposition, and then doing everything possible to nurture it and protect it from the short-term impulse that can corrupt it.

Be transparent.

IT USED TO be that when a baseball umpire made a call, that was it. You could argue, but rarely would he change his mind. Occasionally, he'd go to his fellow umpires for advice, but that was the exception, not the rule.

Now Major League Baseball uses instant replay, allowing them to go to the videotape to make sure they got the call right.

There was a reason for the change, I think, beyond the desire to get the calls right.

Those of us at home, watching on TV, could see more than the umpires could. We were able to see replays from dozens of angles, and we knew—usually beyond a doubt—whether they got it right or not. And when they got it wrong, we all knew it.

Baseball had to adapt, because technology was creating a level of transparency that could threaten the integrity of the game.

That's an important lesson. Technology creates *de facto* transparency for virtually every institution, government, religion, or business.

And these institutions get in trouble when they try to resist transparency, or live under the delusion that they can control the facts or spin the story.

You can't. Not anymore. If you are selling foods that contain genetically modified organisms (GMOs), or clothing that have been made in Asian sweatshops, or cars where it seemed at the time that the company would be better off not doing a recall . . . it is going to catch up with you.

And when it does, you're going to get called "out."

"Values" means one thing.
"Value" means another.

THERE ARE PLENTY of examples of companies that have used positive corporate values as marketing tools to establish themselves with consumers.

Like Tom's, the shoe and eyewear company based in Santa Monica, California. Buy a pair of Tom's shoes, and they give a pair of shoes to a child in need. Buy a pair of eyeglasses, and Tom's uses some of the profits to help people in impoverished areas with eye-related issues, paying for operations that can save or restore their eyesight.

Like Ben & Jerry's, the ice cream manufacturer that was born out of a counterculture attitude in Vermont during the late 1970s. Ben & Jerry's supports environmental causes, opposes the use of rGBH (recombinant bovine growth hormone) in all their products, and recently eliminated the use of all genetically modified ingredients.

Like Starbucks, which from its start provided employees with health care, among other benefits, and recently created a program designed to financially support virtually any employee who wants to get an online college degree from Arizona State University.

These are values statements that go beyond the cost of a pair of shoes, or a pint of ice cream, or a venti latte. They make you feel like the company is more than just a moneymaking enterprise . . . that the dollars you spend there are, in fact, well spent.

Not that value isn't important. In fact, these companies would almost certainly argue that they are providing great value, even if their products are not the cheapest.

But values become value-added.

Value doesn't necessarily mean cheap.

YEARS AGO, I produced a Japanese video documentary about Wegmans, the food retailer serving upstate and western New York with a long and distinguished history. In its home markets, everybody knew someone who had worked at Wegmans, if they hadn't actually worked there themselves. There was great consumer equity built up over decades.

However, as Wegmans expanded into new markets, it did not have that same kind of long-term equity. My Japanese clients wanted to know what people valued most in the Wegmans experience.

We pulled together a focus group of diverse Washington, DC-area shoppers and asked them. We expected them to talk about the things Wegmans was famous for, like its fresh foods and high levels of customer service. But to a person, they said something else: "The prices."

We were blown away. It was the answer we least expected. But this group of people essentially said: "We think the prices on groceries are fair. And the prices on fresh foods may be higher than in other places, but the products are so much better that we feel we are getting much more value for our money."

That's an important lesson about value. Sure, it matters how much the customer spends. But just as important—maybe more important—is what the customer gets back in return.

Anybody can beat you on price.

NO MATTER HOW low you price something, some-one always can undercut you.

That's a rule that superstores and dollar stores have dined out on for the past few years. They figure out what products are price sensitive and do their best to under-price everyone. Which can be an enormous pain in the neck to smaller retailers that don't have the kind of financial infrastructure to support nar-rowing margins. Of course, once the competition has been eliminated, the bigger chains are free to raise their prices a bit. Until the next time or place they need to go nuclear.

This is the best reason in the world for every retailer to find ways to appeal to customers that have nothing to do with price. This isn't to say that

price is not important—especially at a time when price transparency is made possible by technology, and Amazon has algorithms that make it possible to undercut pretty much anybody and everybody on price, should it wish to do so—but it can't be the only thing that is important.

Keep prices as sharp as possible, sure, but find something you can exploit as your differential advantage—the best and freshest doughnuts in the market, or the most unusual colors in a line of shirts, or exceptional customer service, or a frequent shopper program that is really customized and targeted. You have to have *something* that is different, *something* that transcends the price tag, *something* that drives people to the store, even if the guy down the street is a little cheaper.

Cultivate word of mouth.

FIRST, LET'S LOOK at the research . . . in this case, a 2013 Nielsen study of Trust in Advertising, which said that "word of mouth recommendations from friends and family are still the most influential," according to 82 percent of North American consumers. And 68 percent said they trust the opinions of other consumers posted online.

On the other hand, 57 percent said they trust brand sponsorships, and not many more than that trust advertising in traditional media outlets.

This has become more pronounced at a time when a) the amount of advertising out there has reached the point where we cannot distinguish any of the messages amid the clutter, and b) the explosion of social media has created blogs and forums in which actual consumers are candid about their purchases and experiences. "Blogger moms" have developed into an industry of some import for companies that used to depend on television commercials or newspaper ads.

Add to that the fact that many online retailers have embraced the notion of including customer reviews on the pages of products that they sell. Amazon pioneered this, but hardly is alone; online services such as Angie's List and Yelp build their business on customer reviews. Sometimes these reviews are laudatory, often they provide information about styling or sizing that help the shopper make a decision, and frequently they discourage the consumer from making the purchase.

People used to talk about products and services over the back fence or at the water cooler. Word of mouth happens in different places these days, but it remains a powerful sales tool.

Social media is your friend.
Even when it isn't.

THERE ARE A lot of companies that live in fear of social media, because they know that bad stuff—whether it emanates from an employee or a customer—can go viral and have a devastating effect on a business.

A few years ago, a couple of clowns working at Domino's Pizza decided it would be funny to pick their noses, place the effluence on the pizzas they were making, and then videotape the whole thing and post it on YouTube.

Real funny.

The good news is that the employees were fired and then arrested.

The bad news is that when Domino's management learned of the public relations disaster they were facing, their first instinct was to hope that the firestorm would blow over, and their second instinct was to ban all cameras from their kitchens.

What *should* Domino's have done?

Respond. Quickly. Domino's may not have been able to do anything about the tainted pizzas, but the CEO should have quickly let customers know: a) how the company has responded, and b) that he is as outraged as you are. It is critical to be not just a corporate executive in those moments, but a consumer—and say something along the lines of, "I'm a dad, and I often order pizza for my kids. The idea that some idiots would take their responsibilities so lightly is so offensive to me that I almost cannot find the words."

And then, act . . . not by denying the impact of social media, but by embracing it.

Rather than ban cameras from the kitchens, Domino's should have gone the other way, saying, "We are mandating that each and every one of our restaurants offer a refresher course in food safety. I'm letting every one of our restaurants know that we welcome cameras in our kitchens, because we have nothing to be afraid of. This case is a horrible outlier—one that reminds us of how a couple of poor employees can impact our families and our trust. But we are not afraid of further scrutiny. Rather, we welcome it."

Of course, having done all that, you then have to live up to the promise you've made.

Want an example of a company that seems to use social media really well? Zappo's immediately comes to mind—they use e-mail, Facebook, Twitter, and a variety of other social media to create a real relationship with customers. Even if they were to screw up somehow, I suspect that it would not have a lasting impact on business because they've built up considerable equity by talking and listening to their shoppers via social media.

It does no good to fight against the impact of social media. Embrace it, because it can be your friend.

Never give up an advantage.

IN ALMOST EVERY industry, retailers talk about the "level playing field." Especially small retailers, because they say they want the same deals from manufacturers as their bigger brethren.

I think the phrase ought to be struck from the retailing vernacular.

Let's face it—nobody *really* wants a level playing field. They want the advantage. Any advantage. A level playing field suggests parity, and no real competitor wants parity.

Years ago, Priceline, the travel website that created the "name your own price" approach for hotels and airline tickets, decided to expand into groceries.

It developed a "name your own price" program for supermarkets. Customers could decide what they were willing to pay for a can of peas, and then retailers could decide whether to make that deal online, regardless of the shelf price.

This being the early days of e-commerce, a number of retailers signed on for this program. They saw it as their e-commerce strategy at a time when it wasn't clear whether people would buy groceries online.

It didn't last long. Very quickly, retailers picked up on the fact that this was one of the dumbest ideas every created ... because unlike airline seats and hotel beds, that can of peas would be as sellable tomorrow as today. All they were doing by signing onto the Priceline program was creating a level playing field when they'd spent years and tons of money trying to carve out an advantage.

You don't want a level playing field. You want all the differential advantages you can get, and you want the other guy to be playing on *your* home turf, according to *your* rules.

You really don't want it to be a fair fight.

There's no such thing as an unassailable advantage.

THERE WAS A time when it looked like Blockbuster had an unassailable retail advantage in the VHS and DVD rental game. It had stores everywhere, and it was the only national video rental chain of any consequence. Game, set, and match . . .

Except that Blockbuster wasn't paying attention. Netflix, by creating a by-mail rental system that people controlled via their computers, started to eat away at Blockbuster's advantage. Redbox, which put kiosks in supermarkets, convenience stores, and fast food joints, and charged just one dollar a night, had real appeal to parents tired of paying exorbitant late fees for videos their kids left under the sofa. And streaming video, which eliminated the need for a physical DVD, was a threat to the whole rental industry.

If the company had paid attention to what was happening, Blockbuster might exist today. But it didn't. When Blockbuster finally responded to the threats with a change in ownership and strategy, it was too late. What Blockbuster thought of as an unassailable business advantage ended up being an anchor around its neck.

There's always a competitor who can do it better, faster, or cheaper. You always have to be working to figure out the *next* advantage. And the next one after that.

Special is as special does.

THIS RULE CUTS two ways.

It is about how a retailer can make an item special.

And about how shoppers can see even mundane items as special.

Both matter, I think. Because it is in the land of the special where retailers can make a difference.

Years ago, I was working my way through college in an upscale men's clothing store called the British Stock Exchange in Marina del Rey, California. We had a table full of men's cotton lisle knit shirts that were selling for $25. Actually, they weren't selling at all.

My boss, Tim Dyckman, came in one day and ordered me to re-price the shirts, and I asked him how low I should go. Tim shook his head and ordered me to mark them *up* to $40. "At $25, they're just cotton shirts," Tim said. "If they're more expensive, they're something special." I marked them up, and they were gone in a week.

Good lesson, and one I've never forgotten. A smart retailer knows how to treat the products on the shelves as if they are special, not just commodities. And when a product is perceived as special, you've got a lot better shot at making the sale.

The fact is that everything is special to someone.

During the summer months, I team-teach a class at Portland State University's Center for Retail Leadership. Because I want the students to think differently about the consumer packaged goods products we're talking about, I ask them to write an essay about their most memorable meal. It is an easy thing to write about, even if they are not natural writers, and it helps them address the things that are special about food.

The best essay I ever got was from a young man who wrote:

> *My most memorable meal consisted of Minute Rice and A1 Steak Sauce. It was my Christmas dinner.*
>
> *I was in Afghanistan, and we had just returned from patrol, and that is all that was left. But it didn't matter, because I was with my brothers, and they would have died for me, and I would have died for them.*

Not only did that young man get an A+, but he made me think of him every time I see A1 steak sauce and Minute Rice. I used to think of them as commodity products, but now I realize that they are something special, at least to him.

Everything is special to someone. A retailer's job is to find those special points, and then use them to create effective and compelling marketing moments.

Create brand intimacy.

I RECENTLY SAW an interview with Ron Johnson, who ran the Apple Stores from 2000 to 2011. He said something amazing—that only one out of every one hundred visitors to the average Apple Store actually buys anything while there. That's extraordinary, since Apple tends to have the highest sales per square foot in retailing.

Why are people there? Because they are engaged with a brand that they find to be highly connected to their lives. They just want to be around it. It's relevant.

Johnson described it this way: "Bathing in the intimacy between themselves and the brand."

A great brand creates a sense of intimacy with loyal customers, bringing a customer into that brand's worldview to the extent that he or she cannot imagine buying a competitive brand.

Here's an exercise: name three brands that are most relevant to your life. At least one has to be a retail brand.

For me, it is pretty easy—Apple, New Balance, L.L. Bean. (As I write this on my Apple MacBook Pro, I am wearing a shirt and jeans from L.L. Bean and New Balance sneakers. Which is pretty much what I wear every day.) Each of these companies is both manufacturer and retailer. I cannot imagine being outside their ecosystems.

Most of us have those brands, and the great brands create a kind of connectivity that borders on intimacy.

A retailer wants to achieve that level of intimacy with customers, because it creates a level of engagement that prevents people from shopping in other stores.

Some people get it. Some people don't.

During the summer of 2014, Crate & Barrel fired its CEO and brought back the company's founder. The reason: a sense that the classic aesthetic that had informed the company's offerings from the beginning was being diluted by more trendy products that were not in sync with customers' expectations. The retailer's relevance was in question, and its brand intimacy was, well, less intimate.

Lose touch, and you lose customers.

PART THREE

Customers

The boomerang principle.

LET'S RETURN TO Ireland's Feargal Quinn, who is a font of retail wisdom.

In his Superquinn chain of supermarkets, Quinn created a customer service paradigm that had retailers beating a path to Dublin to learn from his example. Quinn sold the chain several years ago and has gone on to a distinguished career of public service in Ireland's Senate. But his "boomerang principle" dates from his early work experience.

Quinn learned the basis for his approach to customer service when he was a kid, working for his father's "holiday camp." Families would book the camp for a week or two, pay one fee, and would have the run of the facilities for the length of their stay. Once that initial fee was paid, no more money

changed hands. The customer service had to be so top-notch that as a family was leaving, the parents would turn to Quinn's father and say, "We had a grand time, Mr. Quinn, and we'll be coming back next year."

In other words, like a boomerang.

Retail success, Feargal Quinn always says, is best measured in how often customers return to the store. And the only way you can come close to guaranteeing that is by making sure they have a grand time while they are there.

Most customers are not out to screw you.

I DON'T KNOW your store, don't know your customers. So I shouldn't say that most of them are not out to screw you. Maybe they are.

But it is a lot easier on the nerves to work on the premise that your customers are essentially honest.

Taking that approach can be a differential advantage. Look at L.L. Bean, which since its inception has had an unconditional anytime-anywhere policy when it comes to returns—it'll take back anything it sells . . . forever.

Even as other companies (REI, for example) have

been stepping back from that approach, L.L. Bean is sticking to its guns. There never has been a meeting at which anyone has questioned whether the guarantee has any value. In fact, Steve Fuller, the company's CMO, says that the only question that gets asked is whether the company talks about it *enough*.

I respect L.L. Bean's position—and not just because L.L. Bean is my idea of a fashion designer. Its policy seems rooted in two ideas retailers need to have: respect for the customer, and a sense that the bottom line is not always served by short-term decision-making.

Knowledge is power.

OR, AS SIR Francis Bacon put it in his 1597 manuscript, "Meditationes Sacrae," *ipsa scientia potestas est*.

Okay, I'll be honest. Despite eighteen years of parochial school education, I know absolutely no Latin. I just knew that there was a Latin translation of "Knowledge is power," so I Googled it and found the Francis Bacon reference.

But this makes my point. Knowledge is more available today than ever, and actionable knowledge can be a powerful ally.

I don't care if you have twenty customers or 20,000. Knowing who they are and what they buy is the single most important weapon you have in providing them with the products they need and the service they want.

It also helps you figure out what they may want in the future, based on habits and past behavior.

There are lots of examples of big companies that do this.

Amazon. Every product you look at, every click you make, is registered and examined by Amazon, which can then, based on those clicks and looks, start to send you information about products that you may be interested in. It's all about algorithms, a science that Amazon has down pat as it tries to steal every customer and every purchase it can.

Or Kroger. It sends out personalized promotional pieces to ten million shoppers on a quarterly/seasonal basis, and is getting a 66 percent response rate. One friend of mine likes to say that they are "weaponizing data," knowing that there is a major war for customers unfolding against the likes of Amazon and Walmart.

This isn't just the purview of big chains.

Nicholas Roberts Fine Wines, a small wine shop near me in Connecticut, started years ago what has become the biggest wine-of-the-month club in the state, despite tons of competition from major chain stores. This has allowed the shop to pay granular attention to what people like and what people buy, so they can build their inventory and promotions accordingly.

And not only should the retailer know as much as possible about customers, but also about the products that it is selling . . . because technology makes it possible for consumers to know as much or more than the retailer does.

You really see this change in the automobile

industry. You used to walk into a dealership with the balance of power tipped toward the salesperson. Today, because of the ability to research everything online, the customer has the power to argue price, options, and availability, and even use the Internet to gather competing offers.

Say it after me: "*Ipsa scientia potestas est.*"

Treat your best customers better than everyone else.

MY DAUGHTER ALI lives at home and commutes to Quinnipiac University. One of the things that keeps her going is Starbucks coffee. She'll often pick up a cup when driving to school, and I think she'd say that for her, it has helped her make the most of the college experience. (She gets terrific grades, so I'm happy to absorb the cost of $4 lattes. Seems like a small investment compared to tuition.)

She has gone to the local Starbucks, in Darien, Connecticut, so often that many of the baristas there know her by name and know what she'll be ordering as soon as she walks through the door. Recently, though, she's been going to the Starbucks closer to school, in Hamden.

I was in the Darien Starbucks getting a cup of coffee. The manager, Nikki, recognized me and asked how my daughter was doing. "She's great," I said. "Her schedule has just been crazy, and now she's taking her finals."

Ali stopped by that Starbucks on her way to school a few hours later, and when Nikki saw her, not only did she make her coffee, but she put a little note on the lid of the coffee cup: "Good luck on finals!" Ali said that the note made her day. And I thought this was really special—this employee connected with one of her customers in a way that transcended the usual.

Sometimes smart retailers need computers and data and all sorts of software. But sometimes, all they need is a smart and savvy employee like Nikki, working with her eyes open and making a difference one customer at a time.

Treat best customers like they matter. They'll stay best customers.

Surprise your customers.

WHEN YOU'RE GOOD, you can take a chance. And when it works, customers will love it.

I was having dinner in Seattle at a place called the Dahlia Lounge. Our server was a young woman named Jacqueline who was funny, attentive (but not overly so), and knowledgable about the menu.

When picking out a wine, I joked about loving adventure—so when I mentioned that I was torn between the Alaskan troll-caught King salmon (with pea shoot-tomato salad, carrot reduction, Yukon gold potatoes, and peas) and the roasted pork loin (with molasses-glazed pork belly, caramelized onion spoon bread, and roasted figs)—she simply smiled, took away my menu, and said she would surprise me.

She did—with the salmon. And it was one of the best salmon dishes I've ever eaten.

Jacqueline knew her stuff, she understood her customers, and she put a great face on an already estimable restaurant. My meal at the Dahlia Lounge was a great food experience . . . in part because Jacqueline embraced the opportunity to surprise me.

(There is a postscript to this story at the end of Rule 38. Read on . . .)

RULE
38

Make every customer a regular.

MORGAN IS THE bartender at Etta's, a fabulous sea-food restaurant overlooking the Pike Place Market in Seattle. I first went into Etta's more than a dozen years ago, sat down at the bar, ordered a glass of wine and some dinner, and engaged in conversation with Morgan. Nothing major, just a chat. The next year back in Seattle on business, I went to Etta's, and Morgan remembered me.

Even though I only get to Seattle a couple times a year, and some years not at all, Morgan always treats me like a regular. I sort of feel like Norm in "Cheers" . . . I walk in, and Morgan greets me by name with a big hello and pours me a glass of wine before I've even settled in my seat, because he knows what I like.

I could hardly be described as a regular, based on the number of times I've been there. Except that I am, because Morgan treats me that way.

There are few things more powerful in the retail experience than making customers feel like regulars. It creates warmth and intimacy and, by the way, sales . . . because people love it. It makes them feel good. It makes them feel welcomed.

And I learned it from Morgan. (By the way, next time you are in Seattle, go to Etta's and ask for Morgan. Tell him Kevin sent you. And order the crab cakes. Trust me.)

Here is the postscript I promised:

Both Etta's and the Dahlia Lounge are owned by the same person—Tom Douglas, one of the best chefs in Seattle. He has a long history of hiring great people, allowing them to do their jobs to the best of their abilities, and rewarding them for their service and loyalty.

Don't mistake bribery for loyalty.

A LOT OF companies, especially big ones, create what they call "loyalty marketing programs," modeled on what the airlines have done so well over the years.

But the majority of these programs are just electronic coupon delivery systems. They do very little to engender any sort of loyalty.

Want proof? Check out your key ring. How many loyalty "fobs" are attached to it? If you're like most people, you have several . . . from competing retailers. You're not loyal. Just opportunistic. Which, as a customer, you have every right to be. Because nobody has given you any reason to be loyal, other than lower prices.

Rather than trying to bribe customers into being loyal by giving them discounts, retailers would be far better off demonstrating their loyalty to the shopper.

Dorothy Lane Markets in Dayton, Ohio, has eliminated all mass advertising, and only communicates with its customers through targeted mailings and e-mailings. Their best customers are really treated like best customers. That goes beyond the targeted offers. Dorothy Lane Markets also hosts dinners and cocktail parties to which only the store's best customers are invited. Sure, it costs money . . . but it's worth it, because those customers aren't going anywhere.

They know that Dorothy Lane Market is loyal to them. That translates to DLM's bottom line.

The customer is always right ... enough.

STEW LEONARD LOVES to tell the story about how, early in his supermarket career, a woman tried to return a carton of eggnog to his store. She said it was bad, but Stew, put off by the accusation, tasted it and said that it wasn't bad. He gave her a replacement carton anyway, but insisted it was fine. The woman then walked away, saying she'd never shop in his store again . . . and he realized that he'd alienated a customer for a carton of eggnog that cost less than a buck.

That led Stew to do something that has helped define his stores. He commissioned the creation of a boulder to stand in front of the store, in Norwalk,

Connecticut, with the following chiseled into it:

> *Our Policy:*
> *Rule 1: The customer is always right!*
> *Rule 2: If the customer is ever wrong, reread*
> *Rule 1.*

That boulder has been replicated outside each of Stew's four stores.

But . . .

The simple fact is—and Stew would almost certainly agree—the customer isn't always right.

The customer just needs to be treated like he or she is right. Because the bottom line is that the customer is always right . . . *enough.*

Alienate the customer, especially these days, and it probably won't just be that one customer who gets the message. Social media makes it possible, even likely, that the message you've sent to the offending customer will be sent to hundreds, thousands, even hundreds of thousands of people.

If you have any doubt, go to your computer and Google "United Breaks Guitars."

And then each time a customer enters your store, imagine that he or she has a dollar sign on his or her forehead. Treat them like they're right . . . *enough.*

Love even the curmudgeons.

A CONSUMER ADVISORY board is a great way to gather input, gauge reactions to new products and services, and test plans and strategies before they're seen by the whole world.

But it is important to make sure that not everybody on the board is a big fan.

At least twenty percent of the people on your board should fall into the "curmudgeon" category, willing to challenge everything and anything you say. Curmudgeons will help stimulate conversation and debate, which is what you want.

Inevitably, because you're going to respect the curmudgeons' points of view and even adopt some of their ideas, they're not going to be so curmudgeonly anymore. They're going to like your company, respect your ideas, and even be nice to you. They're going to become brand ambassadors for you.

Then it's time to get them off the board. And replace them with people not nearly as solicitous.

Rotate the members of your consumer advisory board often. It will keep you from getting complacent.

Listen.

WE RECENTLY BOUGHT a Ford Mustang. Cool car. Makes me feel like Steve McQueen or Spenser every time I sit behind the wheel.

It was not, however, a dream experience. The car came in a month later than expected, and getting information from the dealership was like pulling teeth.

As we (finally) were picking up the Mustang, the salesperson told us that we would be sent a survey asking us to evaluate our experience at the dealership. And she said that if we didn't give her top marks in every category, it would be like failing her.

This makes no sense. She didn't deserve all A's, but she certainly didn't deserve an F. The experience was a C.

The way the survey was structured, it was clear that the dealership didn't actually want to know where she was strong and where she was weak. They didn't want to learn anything. So they put her in the position of asking for an A. When the survey request came in, we ignored it, because we didn't want to lie and we didn't like the rules of the game. So nobody learned anything.

This isn't uncommon.

There's a store where I shop regularly that makes a big deal out of the fact that it listens to and responds to customer suggestions and complaints. There's an enormous suggestion box by the front door. For years, I've been dropping suggestions into that box and including a phone number.

Not once have we ever gotten a phone call. Never.

There's a big difference between saying you listen to customers and asking for their input, and *actually* listening to what they have to say.

One of my kids recently bought a Mini Cooper, and she's been showered with e-mails and phone calls from the dealership. They seem genuinely concerned that she be happy. They offer free car washes to all their customers, which isn't just a nice bonus, but a way of solidifying the customer connection. Whenever she's in the dealership, they're constantly taking her temperature (metaphorically speaking), looking for input about the car.

Soliciting and listening to customer opinions—informally or formally, whether with customer advisory groups or suggestion boxes—is incredibly important. But you actually have to listen, and engage in a dialogue with your shoppers.

If you're not willing to do that, then don't lie about it. That's almost worse.

PART FOUR

Operations

The front lines are where the action is.

UNLESS YOU HAPPEN to be a one or two-store retailer with your name on the door, it is likely that most of your customers have no idea who you are.

But it is entirely likely that they know the person working in checkout lane 3. Or the person staffing their favorite department.

The success or failure of your retail enterprise depends on how engaged your employees are in your business, how clearly they understand your mission, and how they personify your vision in their dealings with customers.

There are retailers out there who "get" it.

Take, for example, Whole Foods, where harmony and service on the sales floor is so important that new hires are voted in or out by other people in the department where they are assigned. If their peers all

agree that they fit in and make the store experience better, they stay. If not, they're shown the door.

Or Nordstrom, where sales associates are empowered to do pretty much anything necessary to ensure that the customer experience is superior, by a management that understands that a store is only as good as the people who work on the front lines.

But I don't think I have to make a list for you. Do it yourself.

Think back to the best experience you've ever had shopping. I'd be willing to bet that moment was based on the way the salesperson interacted with you, facilitating the purchase, making you feel that you were more than just a potential dollar sign.

I'd also be willing to bet that the reason that salesperson behaved that way was that management treated each employee as an asset, not a cost.

A farmer's best fertilizer is his shadow.

IN ANY RETAIL business, leaders need to reserve time to be in the stores.

I'm a big fan of one day a week, though I recognize that this may not always be possible. But on a regular basis, they need to be in the stores, interacting with employees and customers.

When he was CEO of Kroger, Dave Dillon said that walking the floor of stores was one of the ways he stayed in touch with the company's ultimate purpose. A great deal can be learned on location, seeing and hearing the people who work for you and the people who shop with you.

This takes discipline. I know one retail CEO who makes a big deal about spending time on the sales floor, but customers almost never see him there. On the other hand, I know another retail CEO with hundreds of locations around the country, and he visited close to half of them in his first year alone.

Crops can't grow without fertilizer. And a great retail experience cannot thrive unless leadership pays attention with an on-the-ground presence.

The little stuff matters.

I SPEND A lot of time in Portland, Oregon, and one of the great pleasures of being there is going to Stumptown Coffee Roasters. It's a wonderful local coffee shop where on weekends you can wait fifteen to twenty minutes to make your way to the counter, but the coffee is terrific, the ambience is authentic downtown Portland, and the people-watching can be rewarding.

On one recent visit, I ordered my usual—a large nonfat latte. I grabbed a seat at the counter, pulled out my iPad, and started going through e-mail. I kept one eye on the barista and noticed when he seemed to start making what was going to be my latte. A couple of e-mails later, I realized that I had not gotten my coffee, so I took another look . . . and he seemed to

be starting the process all over again. I didn't think too much of it, and went back to my e-mails. Then I noticed when he was done, he took a look, dumped it out, and started over yet again, this time calling over someone to help him.

The third time was the charm, and when he handed me the latte, I couldn't help myself: "I'm just curious. What was wrong with the first two?"

Bo, the fellow who helped, came over and explained that the barista was only several weeks into training and wasn't certified yet. Bo also said that a large nonfat latte was one of the hardest drinks to make—skim milk doesn't hold together the way whole milk or one or two percent milk does. When they get to the end and they're ready to put a design into the foam and it isn't holding together right, they dump it and start over.

Who knew? Then I asked him: "If I'd been getting this to go, and you were putting a top on the cup, would you have gone to all this trouble to make sure the squiggle was right?"

Bo grinned. "It's not worth doing if we can't do it right," he said.

Exactly the right answer. It is just that kind of dedication to excellence that every retailer should be seeking in its employees.

Sometimes we can see the stuff that matters, and sometimes we can't. But it all matters. Even the little stuff.

You have to do it again and again and again.

NORMAN MAYNE IS a retailer of both great taste and humility. For years, he has run Dorothy Lane Markets in Dayton, Ohio, and nurtured their highly deserved reputation as stores where great food is celebrated.

Every year, he brings together the senior management for a retreat, to applaud the success of the past year and discuss the company's plans for the coming year. I asked Norman what he wants them learn from the meeting.

"It's great that we are referred to as a 'legendary' retailer," he said. "But 'legendary' is what we were yesterday. Today and tomorrow and the day after that, we have to go out and earn that all over again."

Smart man. You have to treat today's customers

as if they have no idea how great you were yesterday. What's important is how great you are at this particular moment . . . and then you have to do it again and again and again.

At Dorothy Lane, that means sending employees all over the world seeking out new ideas for prepared meals that will tantalize the senses. Sometimes they find these ideas in stores, but often, they find them in a vineyard or a great restaurant. The goal is to source products nobody else in the market has. It is a task that has resulted in offerings like a Naples-style pizza that is delicious, and not quite like anything you've ever had before. (I've had more than a few slices.)

The great ones like Norman Mayne understand that you have to keep finding new ways to differentiate yourself. It's how they got to be great.

Practice nepotism.

"NEPOTISM" IS DEFINED as "the practice among those in power of favoring relatives or friends, especially by giving them jobs."

Nepotism usually is considered an unhealthy business practice. Which it can be. But not always . . .

As soon as I could begin working legally at the age of 14, I was hired by Dick Coulter to be a salesman and stockboy in his Scarsdale, New York, clothing store, County Boys' and Men's. Dick and his wife Linda were good friends of my parents, and Dick was happy to give me my first job.

He knew that he could count on me . . . because he wasn't my only boss. My parents also had skin in the game, because he was their friend. They went out of their way to make sure that I got to work on time, took all the hours during which he needed me, and even left me home when the family went on vacation during the summer because I had a job, and that was the priority.

Nepotism has gotten a bad rap. There are, of course, plenty of instances when it plays out negatively, especially when people with the right last name get promoted beyond their skills because they happen to be related. But strategic and appropriate nepotism can be a powerful tool.

I developed my work ethic working for Dick Coulter, and to this day I describe Linda and him as my second set of parents. (And I do it with great affection, which is amazing, because most people barely survive one set of parents.)

The tradition continues, by the way. Two of my kids have ended up working for retailers that I've known in different parts of the country. One of them, CEO Kevin Davis of Bristol Farms in Los Angeles, says he loves hiring the kids of people he knows, because those kids are going to work extra hard and be extra dedicated. They have to, because they have two bosses.

Nepotism can work.

The only thing that worries me is this: Kevin Davis has seven kids, and one of these days they might need jobs . . .

Empower employees.

WANT A LESSON in how people on the front lines should be empowered to take care of customer problems?

Simple. Call Amazon next time you have an issue with anything you've bought from them. (That number, by the way, is 1-888-280-4331.)

It is practically guaranteed that whatever the problem, the person on the phone will fix it in a matter of minutes. Without having to go to a supervisor. Without any argument. They'll just send you a new one, or offer you a refund, or do anything you need them to do.

I've experienced this on those rare occasions when I've had problems with an Amazon purchase. Like the time I bought a DVD and it came damaged . . . and the customer service person sent me a new

one overnight, telling me just to send the old one back when I had a chance.

This is because Amazon knows that responding quickly to customer complaints and issues, which means empowering customer service personnel to do what needs to be done and trusting their judgment, is the best way to maintain and nurture sustainable customer relationships.

Challenging the customer, or having to ask a supervisor, simply prolongs a bad situation. And the amount of money involved is almost never worth it.

I know retailers who have told their employees: "You will never, ever get in trouble for trying to make customers happy and for using your discretion to address customer issues. That's what I pay you for."

Those are the retailers I want to patronize.

Trust.

IF IT IS important to empower your employees (Rule 48), you also have to trust them.

In other words, let them know that you trust in their ability to make the best possible decisions they can in the moment (which, by the way, won't always be the *right* decision . . . but that's okay), and won't second-guess them. Later, you might revisit decisions, if only to work through the decision-making process and talk about how to deal with specific situations in the future. But you can't have employees feeling like someone is looking over their shoulders every minute, ready to pass judgment on whether or not they are doing the right thing. Most of them *want* to do the right thing, and, when empowered and trusted, *will* do the right thing.

By trusting your employees, you also are creating an environment in which the people who work for you are going to trust *you*. They know you have their back . . . and they trust you to do the right thing for them.

I worked for three retail bosses who all trusted me, and whom I trusted to treat me well. That's the best kind of environment in which to work.

Hire for attitude.

WHEN YOU ARE hiring a new employee, you want someone who is a) enthusiastic, b) hard-working, and c) personable.

You can teach retailing. You can teach about your products. You can teach about technologies.

But you can't teach attitude.

One company that specializes in employees with great attitude is Trader Joe's. The employees are always friendly and personable. The checkout experience—usually the worst part of any food shopping trip—starts with the cashier asking if you found everything, and often ends with a discussion about what you plan to make with the products you bought.

I know that attitude can be tough to gauge, especially during the interview. Job applicants tend to be on their best behavior.

One way to figure out what kind of attitude an applicant has is to move outside the interview process. See how he or she interacts with other people on the staff. Put the applicant in a position where he or she is chatting with customers. Is he or she friendly? Solicitous? Aloof? What happens when you ask the applicant to pick up a box?

Find ways to find employees who have a great attitude. That's who you want to hire.

There's no such thing as a second first day.

YOU JUST HIRED a new employee on the front lines—a cashier, a sales associate, or a waiter, for example. You know that employee is among the most important people in your company because he or she represents you to your customers.

When the new employee shows up for work the first day, you'd better have someone there as a mentor to begin immersing him or her in the culture of the company and to make sure the employee has something to do and feels productive.

Here are a few things to do on the first day to make a new employee feel like part of the team:

- Issue every new retail employee a stack of business cards with his or her name on them.

- Give the new employee a company e-mail address to which all relevant internal communications will be sent.

- Make sure that the employee has lunch with a supervisor or the store manager along with other employees.

I know a number of young people who have gotten retail jobs, and their first day has proven to be a disappointment. In most cases, things got better, but some of them decided against a career in retail altogether, based on a bad first day. A tremendous opportunity has been lost when that first shift goes by and management hasn't gone out of its way to make it a positive experience.

If you don't make the first day important, you send the message that the employee and his/her job are not important. And the message ought to be exactly the opposite—"you are critical to the success of this retail enterprise, and we want you to feel that in your bones."

The final rule.

WHEN IN DOUBT, throw out the rule book. Or be willing to break the rules (and I'm not just talking about the rules I've offered here, but any rules you've established in your organization).

You have to be willing to break the rules, and empower your people to do so, if that's what it takes to give the customer a better experience.

There will always be times when you have to fly by the seat of your pants, and when rules seem inappropriate, irrelevant, or impossible to implement.

When it happens, try to do the right thing. Not the easy thing. Not the convenient thing. Just the right thing.

Treat your customers the way you'd want to be

treated if you were a customer. Treat your employees the way you wanted or wished your boss had treated you. Treat your business partners in the way you'd expect to be treated by them.

There isn't a rule for every retail situation. So when you can't find one, do the right thing. You won't go wrong.

NOW THAT YOU'VE read all 52 rules (unless, of course, you are one of those people who skips to the end of every book you open), let me suggest that they can be boiled down to five major pieces of guidance:

- Be customer-centric. Always.
- Have a focus.
- Be aggressive.
- Differentiate.
- Have fun.

I think having fun may be the key to great retail. (Think of this as Rule 53.) If the people working in a retail environment are enjoying themselves, that usually translates to how customers will feel about shopping there.

As for those of you who skipped to the end . . . go back and read the whole thing. You can figure out which rules you are following, and which ones you are breaking. Besides, if you don't read the whole thing, you'll never find out where to get the best crab cakes in Seattle, the best coffee in Portland, and why *Jaws* is the perfect business and retailing metaphor.

Trust me.

Acknowledgments

NOT BEING A retailer myself, I have depended on the kindness of many friends for the continuing education that allowed me to write this book. Any list will be woefully incomplete, since I've been doing this for a long time, but let me give it a shot (with apologies for anyone I miss) . . .

Richard and Linda Coulter, Feargal Quinn, Anne and Fiach O'Broin, Jim Donald, Tom Furphy, Glen Terbeek, Norman Mayne, Calvin Mayne, Kevin Davis, Stew Leonard, Stew Leonard Jr., Cathy Burns, Tony Kiser, Tom Gillpatrick, Lauren Johnson, Rudy Dory, Lisa Sedlar, Tim Dyckman, Mike Longo, Tres Lund, Phil Lombardo, Todd Korman, Paul McGillivray, John Cortesi, Danny Rosacci, Mark Anusbigian, Mike Zupan, John Campbell, Kevin Blessing, Larree Renda, Steve Goddard, Dave Dillon, Rich Tarrant, Curt Alpeter, John Lucot, Dan Dmochowski, Mike Burrington, Gerry Lopez, Joanie Taylor, Shelley Broader, Neil and Jane Golub . . . and, of course, the MorningNewsBeat.com community that feeds my mind and my soul every morning. And my appreciation to Neil Raphel and Janis Raye, who came up with the idea for a "Rules" series, asked me to do this one, and then tolerated me through the process.

Finally, thanks to Michael Sansolo and Kate McMahon, who keep MNB from being a lonely pursuit, and Luci Sheehan, who helps to keep the lights on—they prove that despite my reputation, sometimes I do play well with others.